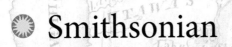
Smithsonian

Exploring
the
North Carolina
Colony

by Jessica Gunderson

CAPSTONE PRESS
a capstone imprint

Smithsonian books are published by Capstone Press,
1710 Roe Crest Drive, North Mankato, Minnesota 56003
www.capstonepub.com

Library of Congress Cataloging-in-Publication Data
Names: Gunderson, Jessica, author.
Title: Exploring the North Carolina Colony/by Jessica Gunderson.
Description: North Mankato, Minnesota: Capstone Press, 2017
Series: Smithsonian. Exploring the 13 Colonies | Includes bibliographical references and index.
Audience: Grades 4–6.
Identifiers: LCCN 2016008942
ISBN 9781515722335 (library binding)
ISBN 9781515722465 (paperback)
ISBN 9781515722595 (ebook PDF)
Subjects: LCSH: North Carolina—History—Colonial period, ca. 1600–1775—Juvenile literature.
Classification: LCC F257 .G86 2017 | DDC 975.6/02—dc23
LC record available at http://lccn.loc.gov/2016008942

Editorial Credits
Jennifer Huston, editor; Richard Parker, designer; Eric Gohl, media researcher;
Kathy McColley, production specialist

Our very special thanks to Stephen Binns at the Smithsonian Center for Learning and Digital Access for
his curatorial review. Capstone would also like to thank Kealy Gordon, Smithsonian Institution Product
Development Manager, and the following at Smithsonian Enterprises: Christopher A. Liedel, President;
Carol LeBlanc, Senior Vice President; Brigid Ferraro, Vice President; Ellen Nanney, Licensing Manager.

Photo Credits
Alamy: Lanmas, 31 (top); Bridgeman Images: © Look and Learn/Private Collection, 23, Service
Historique de la Marine, Vincennes, France, 9; Capstone: 4; The Colonial Williamsburg Foundation: 31
(bottom); Courtesy of Army Art Collection, U.S. Army Center of Military History: 38; Getty Images:
Hulton Archive, 14, 16, 30, 36, Lowell Georgia, 19 (left), National Galleries of Scotland, 32, Stock
Montage, 12, 15, Stringer/MPI, 7, 29; Granger, NYC: 22, 35; Internet Archive: John Carter Brown
Library, 11; iStockphoto: vicm, 19 (right); Library of Congress: 41; New York Public Library: 6, 13,
18, 21; North Wind Picture Archives: cover, 8, 10, 17, 20, 26, 27, 28 (all), 33, 34, 39; SuperStock: 25;
Wikimedia: Public Domain, 5, 19 (middle), 24, 37, 40

Design Elements: Shutterstock

Printed and bound in the USA.
009669F16

Table of Contents

Introduction:
The 13 Colonies

In 1492 Christopher Columbus set sail across the Atlantic Ocean in search of a faster route to Asia. Instead he found what became known as the "New World"—the continents of North and South America. At the time of Columbus' arrival, millions of native people were already living there.

Columbus' voyage kicked off a wave of exploration. Soon more explorers headed to the New World. Some hoped to find a shortcut to Asia. Others were looking for gold and other riches. Explorers from France, the Netherlands, Spain, Portugal, and England also wanted to claim land for their countries.

The land that became North Carolina was once part of the Virginia Colony.

Italian explorer Christopher Columbus was hired by the king and queen of Spain to find a shortcut across the Atlantic Ocean to eastern Asia. Instead he found North America, a land unknown to Europeans at the time.

Spain conquered most of what is now called Latin America, as well as Florida. France claimed much of present-day Canada and set up fur trading posts. In the 1600s England laid claim to what is now the eastern United States.

Settling In

In Jamestown, Virginia, in 1607, England established its first permanent settlement in the New World. By 1733 there were 13 permanent English **colonies** along the eastern coast of North America. A colony is a place settled by people from another country. The new settlement is like a "child" of the old country, which is the "parent" country. The parent country is in charge and makes the rules.

Each of these 13 Colonies had its own unique characteristics. These characteristics were based on who settled there and why. Some were seeking religious freedom—for example, the Puritans in Massachusetts and the Quakers in Pennsylvania. Others simply wanted to get rich off the new land. Many came to farm, and the land and climate determined what they grew. For example, tobacco was grown in Virginia, Maryland, and North Carolina on large farms called plantations. The plantations relied on the labor of **indentured servants** and slaves.

This engraving from the 1800s shows what it may have looked like when the first settlers arrived at Jamestown.

colony—a place that is settled by people from another country and is controlled by that country

indentured servant—a person who works for someone else for a period of time in return for living expenses and travel costs to the colonies

No matter why they came to the New World, the colonists came to stay. They risked their lives crossing the rough waters of the Atlantic Ocean searching for a new life in a new land. They faced hunger, disease, and even death hoping to create a better life for themselves and their families.

A man stands guard while his fellow settlers build a fort at Jamestown in the Virginia Colony.

The Original 13 Colonies

The first permanent European settlement in each colony:

Colony	Year	Colony	Year
Virginia	1607	Delaware	1638
Massachusetts	1620	Pennsylvania	1643
New Hampshire	1623	North Carolina	1653
New York	1624	New Jersey	1660
Connecticut	1633	South Carolina	1670
Maryland	1634	Georgia	1733
Rhode Island	1636		

Chapter 1:
North Carolina's Native People

In 1524 Italian explorer Giovanni da Verrazzano explored the eastern coast of North America. When he spotted land at present-day Cape Fear, North Carolina, he saw campfires along the shore. He realized that people were already living there.

The land that would become North Carolina was home to about 30 native tribes. These tribes spoke one of three languages—Iroquoian, Siouan, and Algonquian.

Native Americans sometimes fished at night. They used spears to catch fish from their canoes.

Did You Know?

When fishing at night, Algonquian tribe members used torches to bring the fish to the surface. When the fish swam toward the light, the fishermen pierced them with spears.

Artist Theodor de Bry based this color engraving of a Native American village on a painting made by colonist John White in the late 1500s.

Algonquian–speaking tribes, such as the Roanokes and Croatoans, lived near the coast. Their houses were rectangular and made of wooden poles and grass mats, topped with arched roofs made of tree bark. Most houses were small, and the entire family lived together in one room. Algonquian villages consisted of about 30 homes surrounded by a wall for protection from wild animals and attacks from enemy tribes.

The Algonquian tribes grew corn, beans, pumpkins, squash, and tobacco. Men, women, and children tended the fields. At harvesttime they celebrated with singing and dancing.

Because they lived near water, fish was a large part of the Algonquian diet. The natives made canoes from hollowed-out tree trunks and caught fish with large nets. They also hunted deer and other game in the nearby forests. They typically used every part of the animals they hunted for food, blankets, and clothing.

To the west of the Algonquian tribes lived the Tuscaroras, an Iroquoian–speaking tribe. The Tuscaroras lived in longhouses—rectangular homes with frames made of tree branches covered with bark. These homes were often quite large, with some measuring 200 feet in length. Many families lived together in one longhouse, although in separate rooms.

Native American longhouses were long, narrow cabins made of tree branches covered with long strips of bark.

Like their Algonquian neighbors, the Tuscaroras grew corn, beans, and squash. They also fished and hunted for deer and smaller animals. Tuscarora women tended the fields. Women also owned all the property. Men often left for months at a time to hunt, fish, or take part in battles.

The Catawbas were the largest Siouan–language tribe. They lived west of the Tuscarora, closer to the Appalachian Mountains. The Catawbas were fierce warriors feared by many tribes. When going into battle, the Catawbas painted their faces with a black circle around one eye and a white circle around the other.

In addition to battling, the Catawba men farmed and hunted. The women wove baskets and made pottery.

Historians believe that the native population of North Carolina numbered more than 100,000 in 1550. But over time, wars and European diseases, such as **smallpox**, would wipe out the once-abundant native people. By 1800 fewer than 20,000 Native Americans remained in North Carolina.

Critical Thinking with Primary Sources

John Lawson helped start two English settlements in North Carolina. In 1709 he published a book describing the landscape and climate of North America and the native people living there. What does the passage below tell you about how the European settlers treated the Native Americans and what they thought of them? How does John Lawson feel about the treatment of the Native Americans?

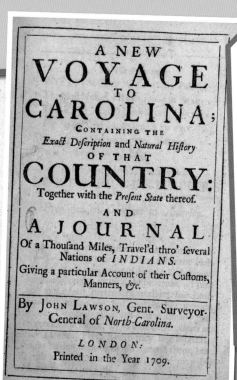

"They are really better to us than we are to them. They always give us Victuals [food] … and take care we are arm'd against Hunger and Thirst … We look upon them with Scorn and Disdain, and think them little better than Beasts in Human Shape … We reckon them Slaves in Comparison to us … [but] these Indians are the freest People in the World … [We] have abandon'd our own Native Soil to drive them out and possess theirs … We trade with them, it's true, but … not to show them the Steps of Virtue and the Golden Rule … No, we … daily cheat them in everything we sell …"

smallpox—a disease that spreads easily from person to person, causing chills, fever, and pimples that scar

Chapter 2:
The Lost Colony of Roanoke

In 1584 Sir Walter Raleigh asked the Queen of England to fund an expedition to America. In July, after nearly two months at sea, two ships reached Roanoke Island off the coast of North Carolina. The explorers met some Native Americans and noticed their abundant crops and rich hunting grounds. When the explorers returned to England, they told Raleigh they'd seen "a most pleasant and fertile ground, replenished with goodly cedars."

Raleigh decided Roanoke Island would be a perfect place for a colony. He named the whole area Virginia and asked his cousin, Richard Grenville, to lead a group of settlers there. In April 1585 Grenville and about 100 men boarded seven ships headed for the New World. They had no idea of the troubles that awaited them.

Sir Walter Raleigh (1554–1618)

Sir Walter Raleigh was an English explorer, adventurer, poet, and politician. He was a favorite of Queen Elizabeth I. From 1584 to 1589, he tried to establish a colony on Roanoke Island in North Carolina. He later searched South America for El Dorado, the fabled city of gold. After Queen Elizabeth's death, Raleigh was accused of plotting against the new king, James I. He was imprisoned in the Tower of London in 1603 and executed in 1618.

Grenville and his men reached the north end of Roanoke Island in July and immediately began building a settlement. They built houses and a walled fort for protection. Meanwhile, Grenville returned to England for supplies.

At first the settlers' relationship with the nearby Algonquians was peaceful. They traded clothing and trinkets for food. But as winter approached, the Algonquians didn't have as much food to spare. Some colonists kidnapped Native Americans and held them captive in exchange for food. When sea captain Sir Francis Drake arrived the following year, he offered to share his supplies with the settlers. Instead they asked him to take them back to England. He did.

Grenville returned to Roanoke Island to find the fort abandoned. He left 15 men behind to maintain the fort and returned to England.

Richard Grenville

13

Try, Try Again

Despite this failure Raleigh was determined to set up a permanent colony. He organized a second expedition to Roanoke Island and named John White as governor of the colony. White, along with 116 men, women, and children, set off for Roanoke Island in 1587. They hoped to meet up with the men Grenville had left there. But when they reached the fort, they saw an eerie sight. The fort had burned down, and most of the buildings were destroyed. They found the bones of one man but no sign of the others. They had disappeared.

The colonists moved into some of the remaining houses and rebuilt others. White sailed to England in late August to gather more supplies. But due to a war with Spain, it would be three years before White could return to Roanoke Island.

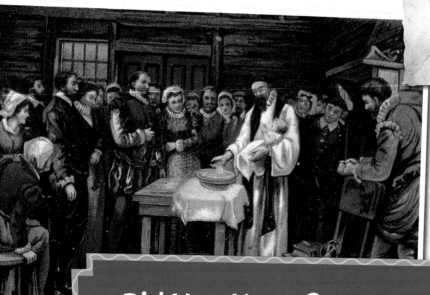

The baptism of Virgina Dare, the first child born to English parents in America.

Did You Know?

John White's granddaughter—Virginia Dare—was the first English child born in America. She was born on Roanoke Island just a few months after the colonists arrived. A week after Virginia was born, John White returned to England for supplies. No one knows what became of Virginia Dare, her family, or the other lost colonists.

John White and his crew used clues to try to figure out what happened to the missing colonists.

When White finally returned, he found the fort abandoned and the houses taken apart. Trees had been chopped down and placed in a circle. The letters "CRO" were carved into the trunk of one large tree. White explored further and saw the word "CROATOAN" etched on the fort's gatepost.

White assumed the colonists had fled to nearby Croatoan Island where a group of friendly Native Americans lived. He set sail for the island, but a storm blew him off course. He returned to England without ever knowing what became of his colony. To this day the lost colony of Roanoke remains a mystery. Some historians believe Native Americans attacked the colony and killed all the settlers. Others believe the colonists may have run out of food and taken shelter with the Croatoans.

England waited nearly two decades to attempt another colony in America. In 1607 Jamestown, Virginia, became the first permanent English settlement in America.

Chapter 3:
The Colony Grows

In Jamestown and other parts of Virginia, many colonists learned how to grow tobacco from the Native Americans. The colonists shipped the tobacco to England where it was sold. As Virginia grew some colonists settled south of Jamestown in what later became North Carolina. But for the most part, the Carolina region remained unsettled by Europeans.

In 1663 King Charles II granted eight men, called Lords **Proprietors**, a **charter** to control Carolina. These men were given the authority to build settlements, organize armies, and collect taxes. At that time Carolina consisted of all or parts of the present-day states of North Carolina, South Carolina, and Georgia.

To attract settlers the proprietors, or landlords, gave a large area of land to each person who settled in Carolina. The proprietors also promised religious freedom.

Everyone pitched in when it was time to harvest the tobacco crop.

> *"We will grant . . . freedom and liberty of conscience in all religious or spiritual things."*
>
> —A Declaration and Proposals of the Lord Proprietor of Carolina, 1663

In Colonial times farmers used large barrels to transport tobacco to port cities where it was shipped to England for sale.

Most of Carolina's colonists came from Virginia and started small farms or larger tobacco plantations. However, the northern Carolina coast was rugged and had no good ports. As a result tobacco farmers took their crops to port towns in Virginia to be shipped to England. Many farmers also sold their tobacco within the colonies.

The Navigation Act of 1660 required that Colonial goods be sold to England and carried on English ships. Later the Plantation Duty Act of 1673 imposed a tax on all colony-to-colony sales of certain goods, such as tobacco, cotton, and sugar. These two acts enraged the Carolina farmers and plantation owners. They wanted to be able to sell their goods without having to pay fees or taxes. Many farmers ended up selling their goods to **smugglers** to avoid the tax.

proprietor—a person given ownership of a colony

charter—an official document granting permission to set up a new colony, organization, or company

smuggler—a person who sneaks illegal goods into or out of a country

Troubled Times

In 1677 a group of colonists revolted against the Navigation Acts. John Culpeper and George Durant led a group of about 40 armed men to the home of Governor Thomas Miller. They stormed the house, arrested him, and put him in jail. The colonists then made John Culpeper the governor. He served for two years before the proprietors removed him from office.

Because of the trouble Culpeper's Rebellion caused, the proprietors realized Carolina needed a stronger government. In 1691 they made Philip Ludwell governor of the Carolina colony. But Ludwell lived in Charles Town, in the southern part of Carolina. As a result he chose a **deputy** governor for the northern part of the colony. This system satisfied the colonists, but a new rebellion was about to begin.

In the late 1670s, Governor Thomas Miller charged the Carolina colonists hefty fees. Fed up with these fees and taxes placed on them by Britain's **Parliament**, several colonists arrested Governor Miller (fourth from right) and threw him in jail.

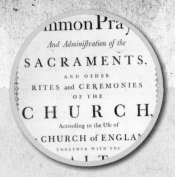

Catholics: Catholics believe in the teachings of the Bible as they are interpreted by the Catholic Church. The pope is the leader of the Catholic Church.

Anglicans: In the 1500s Protestantism—a branch of Christianity—was formed to challenge the Catholic Church. Protestants believe that the teachings of the Bible did not need to be interpreted by the Catholic Church. In 1534 King Henry VIII made Anglicanism, a form of Protestantism, the official Church of England. He also made himself the head of the Anglican Church.

Puritans: Puritanism began as an offshoot of the Anglican Church. However, Puritans believed that the Church of England was too similar to the Catholic Church. Puritans wanted to strip or "purify" their church of all similarities to Catholicism. Most Puritans also believed that each person and each congregation was responsible to God not to the King of England.

Loyalty by Force

Many settlers came to Carolina seeking religious freedom. In England all citizens had to be members of the Anglican Church. Many religious groups, including the Quakers and the Puritans, didn't like this. They felt that the Anglican Church was too much like the Catholic Church. Some also didn't like that the king of England was the head of the Anglican Church. Many people left England to settle in America where they hoped to practice their faith in peace.

deputy—an assistant law enforcement officer
Parliament—Great Britain's lawmaking body

Although the proprietors originally promised religious freedom, that changed in the early 1700s. In 1701 a law was passed requiring all colonists to pledge their loyalty to the Anglican Church. This new law angered Quakers, who refused to take the oath.

At first Thomas Cary, the deputy governor of the northern part of Carolina, insisted that all colonists take the oath. But he changed his mind when he realized he needed the support of Quakers to keep his job. Instead he removed the oath requirement and **appointed** many Quakers to government positions.

In the early 1700s, Quakers who refused to join the Anglican Church—such as the man and woman shown here—could be sent to jail.

In June 1711, Thomas Cary and a group of armed men attempted to raid Edward Hyde's home. But when they saw that he had received extra weapons and manpower, they backed down.

In late 1710 the proprietors made Edward Hyde the deputy governor of northern Carolina. Hyde planned to enforce the oath of loyalty to the Anglican Church. Thomas Cary and his supporters refused to acknowledge Hyde as deputy governor and would not take the oath.

Angered, Hyde gathered a force of 150 men to attack Cary's home. But Cary had fled to a nearby house. When Hyde's group tracked down Cary and saw that he had 40 men and five cannons on his side, they retreated.

Cary then organized an attack on Hyde's forces. By this time Hyde had received **reinforcements**, and Cary was beaten back. Cary's Rebellion had failed. Afterward Quakers were banned from serving in the government.

appoint—to choose someone for a job
reinforcements—additional troops sent into battle

Chapter 4:

Conflicts in North Carolina

As North Carolina became more populated, new settlers moved south to fertile farmlands. In 1695 English settlers established the town of Bath. In 1710 Swiss and German colonists nearby founded the town of New Bern. This settlement was in the heart of the Tuscarora hunting grounds. The residents of New Bern traded with the nearby Tuscaroras but often made unfair deals. Some settlers even kidnapped Tuscarora people and sold them as slaves to work on tobacco farms.

The Tuscarora War

In September 1711 the Tuscaroras declared war on the colonists. They hoped to regain their hunting grounds by pushing the colonists out of the region. The Tuscaroras organized small groups of warriors to attack nearby towns and plantations. More than 130 colonists were killed, including John Lawson, a cofounder of Bath and New Bern. Many women and children were captured.

The Tuscarora people went to war with the Carolina colonists in hopes of getting their hunting grounds back.

Carolina Governor Edward Hyde asked for help from Virginia and South Carolina. In January 1712 Colonel John Barnwell of South Carolina led a force of 30 soldiers and 500 Native Americans to the Tuscarora town of Narhantes. They set fire to the town and killed 52 Tuscaroras.

Soon after the Tuscaroras agreed to stop fighting. But the peaceful times did not last. Battles continued to break out between the colonists and the Tuscaroras. In one notable battle, Captain James Moore of South Carolina led white settlers and a group of Native American warriors to the Tuscarora fort of Neoheroka. Moore's forces killed or captured about 950 Tuscaroras. Several others surrendered. After the war many Tuscaroras left the Carolina region for northern New York to live with the Iroquois.

With the help of Native American warriors, Captain James Moore's troops defeated a large group of Tuscaroras and brought the war to an end.

Villains on the Seas

After the Tuscarora War, the colonists had another problem to deal with—pirates. All along the Carolina coast, pirates attacked and robbed merchant ships. With its many islands and inlets, the Outer Banks of North Carolina became a great place for pirates to hide.

The most famous pirate was an Englishman named Edward Teach, better known as Blackbeard. Standing over 6 feet tall with a long jet-black beard, he looked quite fierce. To make himself look even more frightening, he placed lit matches in his hair.

In 1718 Lieutenant Robert Maynard of the British Navy vowed to stop Blackbeard from seizing ships and terrorizing the seas. Maynard sailed to Ocracoke Island, where Blackbeard's ship was anchored. When Blackbeard saw Maynard coming, his men fired their guns at the British sailors.

Edward Teach was better known as the pirate Blackbeard.

Thinking that they'd won the battle, Blackbeard and his men stormed the ship. Suddenly Maynard and several of his men appeared from below deck, and a hand-to-hand fight broke out. When Maynard shot Blackbeard in the shoulder, the wounded pirate staggered toward him. Before Blackbeard could reach Maynard, a British sailor slashed the pirate's throat.

After the death of Blackbeard, piracy declined. Even though some pirates still prowled the coast, none was as feared as Blackbeard.

In 1718 Blackbeard was killed in a dramatic battle with Robert Maynard of the Royal Navy.

Stede Bonnet: The "Gentleman Pirate" (1688–1718)

Stede Bonnet was not a typical pirate. He was known as the "gentleman pirate" because he came from a wealthy family and was well educated. He was a retired British Army major who owned a successful sugar plantation in Barbados. It is unclear why he left his wife and young children and turned to a life of crime as a pirate.

After spending some time with Blackbeard, Bonnet raided ships along the Carolina and Virginia coasts. In a short time, he became a ruthless pirate in his own right.

Bonnet was captured off the Carolina coast in 1718. He and his crew were taken to Charles Town, South Carolina, where they were later hanged.

Chapter 5:
Colonial Life in North Carolina

After a rocky start to the 18th century, peace and stability came to the Carolina region. However, the colonists were not happy with the job that the proprietors were doing, and they let the king know. So in 1719 King George I bought South Carolina from the proprietors and turned it into a **royal colony**. This meant that it was ruled directly by the king. In 1729 the king took control of North Carolina as well. Under the king's rule, the population of North Carolina grew.

Because of conflicts with Native Americans, Colonial settlers took turns standing guard while others tended the crops.

North Carolina's abundance of land and its booming tobacco and lumber trade drew **immigrants** from Europe and the other American Colonies. Germans, Welsh, Scots, and Irish were among the many settlers. They formed communities across North Carolina, where they kept their customs and culture alive.

Daily Life for North Carolina Colonists

Most colonists in North Carolina were farmers. They grew corn, wheat, and peas and raised cows, horses, and pigs. Farmers sold their extra crops and livestock to neighboring towns or to England. Farm families lived in small wooden houses that had one or two rooms on the ground floor and an area for sleeping upstairs.

At a very young age, children were required to help with chores. Boys milked cows, planted crops, and helped with the harvest. Girls helped their mothers cook, sew, and tend the garden. Most farm children didn't attend school. Parents taught them to read and write at home.

Children had very little time to play. They typically had one or two handmade toys, such as dolls, spinning tops, balls, and clay marbles. They also played outdoors, climbing and running races.

Critical Thinking with Primary Sources

This image shows a young Colonial girl churning butter, a typical chore for children. What does this picture tell you about the lives of Colonial children? Why do you think Colonial families relied upon their children to help run the household? How do the chores of Colonial children differ from chores in today's homes?

royal colony—a colony controlled by a monarch or his representatives

immigrant—a person who moves from one country to live permanently in another

Some North Carolina colonists were merchants or tradespeople. Merchants owned stores or businesses in the colony's small towns, selling food, clothing, or other goods. Tradespeople provided services such as carpentry or blacksmithing. Children in towns often attended public schools. Some children became apprentices and were taught a trade or craft.

North Carolina had a few wealthy colonists who owned large tobacco plantations. They lived in grand houses with high ceilings and fancy furniture from England. Wealthy children were educated by private tutors and sent to college in Europe.

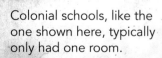

Colonial schools, like the one shown here, typically only had one room.

Young boys often worked as apprentices to master craftsmen, such as the woodworker shown here.

Indentured servants learned trades—such as making bricks—that they could use when their service was up.

Forced Labor

Indentured servants were also common in North Carolina. In exchange for passage to America, indentured servants worked for farmers or tradesmen for several years. After their service was up, indentured servants were free to purchase a farm or start a business.

Plantation owners relied heavily upon slaves. Slavery had existed in North Carolina since the 1680s and grew rapidly in the 1700s. Most slaves were people from Africa who had been kidnapped and sold into slavery. Slave ships carried them from Africa to the colonies.

Conditions on slave ships were terrible, and many people did not survive the journey to America. Those who did survive were sold to slave masters.

Most slaves worked in the tobacco fields, planting, tending, and harvesting crops. Other slaves worked in the home, cooking, cleaning, and caring for the master's children. Most slaves were expected to work six days a week, from sunrise to sunset. They were often beaten with whips or chains if they worked too slowly or if they made their masters unhappy. Children born to slaves were also slaves and were considered the owner's property. They were expected to work starting at a young age. Children often cooked, cleaned, and tended gardens. Slave children could be sold and taken away from their families at any time.

Slave families lived in small, one-room houses with dirt floors. Some grew their own vegetable gardens. When they were finished with a long day of the master's work, the slaves returned to their quarters to do their own chores.

Most slaves lived in tiny shacks on plantations.

Slaves tried to keep many of their African customs. They spoke their native languages, sang traditional African songs, and played African instruments. When a child was born, the slaves gathered to hold a naming ceremony for the baby. The slaves had to keep these customs secret. They could be severely punished if their master found out.

In 1712 about 800 slaves lived in North Carolina. By 1767 that number had grown to 40,000. After slave rebellions in other colonies, North Carolina residents became fearful that the growing slave population would overthrow them. Beginning in 1715 the leaders of North Carolina passed laws called slave codes that further restricted the freedom of slaves. For example, slaves were not allowed to gather in groups, even to worship. Slave owners hoped these rules would prevent slave rebellions.

Harvesting tobacco was backbreaking work that slaves were forced to perform.

Critical Thinking with Primary Sources

This advertisement appeared in a North Carolina newspaper in 1775. It asks for the capture and return of a runaway Native American slave. What does this advertisement tell you about the rights of slaves during Colonial times?

BUTE County, *North Carolina, March 20, 1775.*

RUN away from the Subfcriber, a Slave of the *Indian* Breed, a tall flim made Fellow, with long ftraight black Hair, about 23 Years of Age, had on, when he went away, a blue Duffil Waiftcoat, old Check Shirt, &c, but fince he left me has fold fundry Goods; fo that he may have changed his Drefs. He is branded on both Cheeks, with the letter R on the right, and the letter T on the left. It is fuppofed he will make for *Prince George* County in *Virginia,* or to fome feaport Town on James River. Whoever fecures him in any of his Majefty's Gaols, fo that I may get him again, fhall have 40 s. Reward, to be paid R the Gaoler. The Brands on his Cheeks were frefh given him by the Perfon of whom I bought him, and were not cured when he left me, WILLIAM TABB.
✱✱ All Perfons are forewarned employing or harbouring the faid Slave, at their Peril.

Chapter 6:
The Rise to Rebellion

In 1754 Great Britain went to war with France over control of lands in North America. Some Native American tribes fought with the French, while others backed the British. The colonists fought for Britain.

The British won the French and Indian War in 1763. However, they scrambled to find money to pay for it. King George III decided to raise taxes on the American colonists to pay for the war. The British imposed the Stamp Act in 1765, which required colonists to purchase a stamp for all printed documents. The Stamp Act was later **repealed**, but additional taxes on sugar, tea, and other everyday items made the colonists furious. They believed they should not pay taxes unless they were allowed to participate in the government. They wanted a say in any political decisions that affected their daily lives.

Great Britain's King George III

Many colonists were angry about the Stamp Act. Some newspapers placed a skull and crossbones where the stamp should go.

During this time men throughout the 13 Colonies joined Sons of Liberty groups to protest the Stamp Act and other taxes. North Carolina's group was one of the most active. North Carolina's Sons of Liberty group organized **boycotts** of stamped goods and held a mock funeral for "Liberty." In Wilmington, North Carolina, an angry mob frightened stamp master William Houston into resigning his post. The Sons of Liberty were largely responsible for preventing the Stamp Act from being enforced in North Carolina.

Fighting Back in the Backcountry

Meanwhile, tensions were building between the colonists in the eastern and western parts of North Carolina. Life was very different for western colonists than for eastern colonists. Those in the west lived on the frontier, also called the backcountry. They often struggled to make a living. Eastern colonists controlled the Colonial government and were generally wealthier. Western colonists were angry about the power the east had over them. They felt the politicians in the east were dishonest and were making them pay extra taxes.

repeal—to officially cancel something, such as a law

boycott—to refuse to buy or use a product or service to protest something believed to be wrong or unfair

In North Carolina's backcountry, a group of colonists decided to fight back. The group, known as the Regulators, refused to pay the taxes. They also distributed pamphlets and protested government **corruption**.

For the most part, the Regulators' actions were nonviolent. That changed on May 16, 1771, when Governor William Tryon sent a **militia** to put an end to the Regulators' protests. On that day nearly 2,000 Regulators met up with 1,000 of Tryon's men near Great Alamance Creek in north-central North Carolina. The Regulators asked to discuss their grievances with Governor Tryon. He refused and gave them an hour to surrender. When they did not, Tryon ordered the militiamen to fire their cannons at the Regulators. The backcountry farmers, who were not as skilled in battle as the militiamen, surrendered after a two-hour skirmish.

Several Regulator leaders were captured and hanged. Afterward many Regulators moved away from North Carolina. Despite the Regulators' defeat, their ideas help lay the groundwork for a bigger revolution to come.

Governor Tryon (left center with arm raised) argues with a group of Regulators.

> *"Now [show] yourselves to be Freemen, and for once assert your Liberty and maintain your Rights!"*
>
> —Regulator leader Herman Husband, in a 1769 pamphlet

Penelope Pagett Barker (1728–1796)

Penelope Barker is famous for her role in organizing a protest against unfair British taxes. She was a wealthy woman who lived in Edenton, North Carolina. Angered by Britain's "taxation without representation," Barker wrote a public statement calling for boycotts of British products. On October 25, 1774, she gathered a group of 50 other women to meet at the home of Elizabeth King for a "tea party." There the women signed a pledge to boycott British goods, including tea. Barker sent the proclamation to a London newspaper. The British did not take the proclamation seriously, but throughout the 13 Colonies, many women followed suit. The Edenton Tea Party, as it became known, was one of the first times women in the American Colonies took an active role in politics.

North Carolina Citizens Unite

Although the Regulators had been shut down, resentment and anger toward the Colonial government lingered. Finally in August 1774, North Carolina's leaders drafted a document listing all the British taxes and policies they objected to. They called themselves the Provincial Congress.

North Carolina's new governor, Josiah Martin, sided with the British and opposed the actions of the Provincial Congress. Even so, protests against the British government continued. Colonists formed militia groups to prepare for war with Great Britain. They also sent delegates to a meeting of the colonies called the First Continental Congress. Fearing for his safety, Governor Martin left North Carolina.

corruption—dishonest behavior

militia—a group of volunteer citizens who are organized to fight but are not professional soldiers

Chapter 7:
War and the Road to Statehood

On April 19, 1775, the Revolutionary War began in Massachusetts with battles between American **Patriots** and British soldiers. But in North Carolina and other colonies, not everyone wanted independence from England. Some colonists, known as **Loyalists**, believed they were better off under British rule. In the War for Independence, many Loyalists fought alongside British soldiers.

The War Comes to North Carolina

In February 1776 some Patriot militiamen learned that a group of Loyalists was planning to march through Wilmington, North Carolina, across Moores Creek Bridge. The Patriots removed some planks from the bridge and waited. When the Loyalists attempted to cross the bridge, some fell into the water. The Patriots charged, firing their muskets and cannons. Within minutes the surprised Loyalists retreated. The Patriots had won the first battle in North Carolina.

Patriots and Loyalists faced off at the Battle of Moores Creek Bridge.

A Case of Mistaken Identity

Only a handful of battles were fought in North Carolina until early 1781. On February 24 Continental army officers Andrew Pickens and Henry Lee were on a mission to track down and ambush the enemy. As they made their way through the North Carolina wilderness, Lee's troops encountered two men from a Loyalist regiment led by Colonel John Pyle. Some of Lee's men were wearing green coats, rather than the blue jackets typically worn by the Continental army. Pyle's men mistakenly thought they were members of Colonel Banastre Tarleton's British Legion, who wore similar uniforms. Lee realized that he could use this case of mistaken identity to his advantage.

British Colonel Banastre Tarleton

Mary "Polly" Slocumb (1728–1796)

On the night before the Battle of Moores Creek, Mary Slocumb had a disturbing dream. She saw a body wrapped in her husband Ezekiel's coat, which was covered in blood. She awoke in a panic, got dressed, and took off on horseback. She needed to find out if Ezekiel, a member of the North Carolina militia, was dead or alive.

Mary rode 30 miles throughout the night, finally arriving near Moores Creek while the battle was still raging. She quickly found the spot she saw in her dreams. She did find a man wrapped in a bloody coat, but he was not dead, and he wasn't her husband.

Mary was relieved to hear that her husband was alive and well, fighting the enemy close by. Like many women at the time, Mary spent the day nursing the wounded on the battlefield. Her actions that day saved many lives. She returned home that night after seeing her husband.

Patriot—a person who sided with the colonies during the Revolutionary War

Loyalist—a colonist who was loyal to Great Britain during the Revolutionary War

The next day Lee and his green-clad soldiers came upon the rest of Pyle's troops. Lee and Pyle exchanged greetings and shook hands. Lee's trickery had worked. He had even fooled Colonel Pyle.

Lee's men quickly drew their swords and slaughtered Pyle's men. Pyle's Loyalist troops were so taken by surprise that they cried out, "You are killing your own men!"

Confused by what was happening, 93 of Pyle's men were dead within 10 minutes. Many were injured, some were taken prisoner, and a few managed to escape.

American General Nathanael Greene leads his troops against the British at the Battle of Guilford Courthouse.

A Strategic Victory

At the town of Guilford Courthouse (present-day Greensboro, North Carolina) on March 15, 1781, British General Charles Cornwallis advanced upon Continental troops. General Nathanael Greene led the Continentals—a group of nearly 4,500 soldiers and militiamen. Cornwallis' men numbered just 1,900.

After more than two hours of gunfire and fierce hand-to-hand combat, Greene ordered his troops to retreat. Greene meant this as a strategic move, not as a sign of defeat. He knew his men had already severely weakened Cornwallis' army, so he didn't want to risk their lives any further.

After the Battle of Guilford Courthouse, Cornwallis gave up his campaign in the Carolinas and headed to Virginia. At Yorktown, Virginia, in October of that year, General George Washington's Continental troops surrounded Cornwallis' men and forced them to surrender. This was the last major battle of the war.

British General Charles O'Hara gives General Cornwallis' sword to American General Benjamin Lincoln as a token of surrender after the Battle of Yorktown.

"I never saw such fighting since God made me. The Americans fought like demons."
—General Charles Cornwallis describing the Battle of Guilford Courthouse

The Road to Statehood

With the war over, the United States was officially recognized as an independent nation. As such, the new country needed a permanent system of government. On September 17, 1787, **delegates** from 12 of the 13 Colonies signed the U.S. Constitution in Philadelphia. (Rhode Island did not send representatives to the Constitutional Convention.)

Three delegates from North Carolina signed the U.S. Constitution. But each state also needed to **ratify** it in order to join the United States. At first North Carolina's delegates refused to ratify the Constitution because some felt that it did not do enough to protect the rights of individuals. Then in 1789 Congress agreed to add the Bill of Rights to the Constitution. These ten **amendments** to the Constitution guarantee Americans certain rights, such as freedom of speech and freedom of religion. With the addition of the Bill of Rights, North Carolina approved the Constitution and became the 12th state.

George Washington (standing right) watches as delegates from the 13 Colonies sign the U.S. Constitution.

For its capital city, North Carolina chose the central location of Raleigh. The town was named for Sir Walter Raleigh, the man who had the vision to colonize North Carolina so many years before.

This 11-foot statue of Sir Walter Raleigh is located in downtown Raleigh, the capital city of North Carolina.

Did You Know?

After the Revolutionary War, many states needed to pay off war debts. As a result North Carolina offered Congress several million acres of land in the western part of the state. This idea angered people already living in the area. In 1784 they declared independence from North Carolina and called themselves the State of Franklin. Franklin asked Congress to become the 14th state but was rejected. Even so, Franklin remained independent for four years before rejoining North Carolina. The land became part of Tennessee when that state was formed in 1796.

delegate—someone who represents other people at a meeting

ratify—to formally approve a document

amendment—a formal change made to a law or legal document, such as the U.S. Constitution

Timeline

1492 Christopher Columbus reaches the New World.

1524 Giovanni da Verrazano lands at Cape Fear, North Carolina.

1584 Sir Walter Raleigh receives funding for an expedition to North America.

1585 Roanoke Island's first colony is established but is abandoned a year later.

1587 Governor John White establishes a second colony on Roanoke Island.

1590 John White returns to Roanoke Island to find no trace of the colonists he left behind three years earlier.

1607 Jamestown, Virginia, becomes the first permanent English settlement in North America.

1663 King Charles II gives eight men a charter to control Carolina.

1673 The Plantation Duty Act places a tax on sales of certain goods sold between the colonies.

1677 Colonists wage Culpeper's Rebellion in protest of Plantation Duty taxes. Culpeper serves as governor for two years.

1701 The proprietors pass an act requiring all colonists to take an oath of allegiance to the Anglican Church.

1705 Bath becomes the first town in North Carolina.

1710 The proprietors divide Carolina into two colonies—North and South Carolina—with separate governments.

1718 Robert Maynard kills the pirate Blackbeard off the shore of North Carolina.

1729 North Carolina becomes a royal colony.

1754 The French and Indian War begins.

1763 The French and Indian War ends with a British victory. France surrenders most of its land in North America.

1765 The British Parliament passes the Stamp Act to help pay its war debt.

1771 The North Carolina militia clashes with the Regulators.

1774 North Carolina leaders meet for the Provincial Congress and send delegates to the First Continental Congress.

1775 The Revolutionary War begins with the Battles of Lexington and Concord in Massachusetts.

1776 Patriots defeat Loyalists at the Battle of Moores Creek Bridge in North Carolina.

1781 Patriots attack British troops under General Cornwallis at Guilford Courthouse. Cornwallis later surrenders at Yorktown, Virginia.

1783 Great Britain and the United States sign the Treaty of Paris, officially ending the Revolutionary War. The United States is officially recognized as an independent nation.

1787 Three North Carolina delegates sign the U.S. Constitution.

1789 North Carolina becomes the 12th state to ratify the Constitution.

Glossary

amendment (uh-MEND-muhnt)—a formal change made to a law or legal document, such as the U.S. Constitution

appoint (uh-POINT)—to choose someone for a job

boycott (BOY-kot)—to refuse to buy or use a product or service to protest something believed to be wrong or unfair

charter (CHAR-tuhr)—an official document granting permission to set up a new colony, organization, or company

colony—(KAH-luh-nee)—a place that is settled by people from another country and is controlled by that country

corruption (kuh-RUP-shuhn)—dishonest behavior

delegate (DEL-uh-guht)—someone who represents other people at a meeting

deputy (DEP-yuh-tee)—an assistant law enforcement officer

immigrant (IM-uh-gruhnt)—a person who moves from one country to live permanently in another

indentured servant (in-DEN-churd SERV-uhnt)—a person who works for someone else for a period of time in return for living expenses and travel costs to the colonies

Loyalist (LOI-uh-list)—a colonist who was loyal to Great Britain during the Revolutionary War

militia (muh-LISH-uh)—a group of volunteer citizens who are organized to fight but are not professional soldiers

Parliament (PAHR-luh-muhnt)—Great Britain's lawmaking body

Patriot (PAY-tree-uht)—a person who sided with the colonies during the Revolutionary War

proprietor (proh-PREYE-uh-ter)—a person given ownership of a colony

ratify (RAT-uh-fye)—to formally approve a document

reinforcements (ree-in-FORSS-muhnts)—additional troops sent into battle

repeal (ri-PEEL)—to officially cancel something, such as a law

royal colony (ROI-uhl KAH-luh-nee)—a colony controlled by a monarch or his representatives

smallpox (SMAWL-poks)—a disease that spreads easily from person to person, causing chills, fever, and pimples that scar

smuggler (SMUHG-lur)—a person who sneaks illegal goods into or out of a country

Critical Thinking Using the Common Core

1. Describe the reasons immigrants from other colonies and Europe settled in North Carolina. Compare and contrast the various reasons. (Integration of Knowledge and Ideas)

2. Were the Tuscarora people justified in waging war against the colonists? Why or why not? Use details from the text to support your answer. (Key Ideas and Details)

3. If you could take a time machine back to Colonial America, would you? Why or why not? (Integration of Knowledge and Ideas)

Read More

Blake, Kevin. *Roanoke Island: The Town That Vanished*. Abandoned!: Towns Without People. New York: Bearport Publishing, 2014.

Buckley, James, Jr. *Who Was Blackbeard?* New York: Grosset & Dunlap, 2015.

Garstecki, Julia. *Life in Colonial America*. Daily Life in U.S. History. Minneapolis: Core Library, 2015.

Jeffries, Joyce. *The Colony of North Carolina*. Spotlight on the 13 Colonies. New York: PowerKids Press, 2015.

Internet Sites

FactHound offers a safe, fun way to find Internet sites related to this book. All of the sites on FactHound have been researched by our staff.
Here's all you do:
Visit *www.facthound.com*
Type in this code: 9781515722335

Check out projects, games and lots more at
www.capstonekids.com

45

Source Notes

Page 11, primary source box: John Lawson, *A New Voyage to Carolina*. London: 1709, pp. 235–236. Accessed April 18, 2016, https://archive.org/stream/newvoyagetocarol00laws#page/n3/mode/2up.

Page 12, line 6: Richard Hakluyt, *Voyages of the Elizabethan Seamen to America: Thirteen Original Narratives*, ed. E. J. Payne (London: Thomas De La Rue & Co., 1880), p. 220.

Page 17, callout quote: "A Declaration and Proposals of the Lord Proprietor of Carolina, Aug. 25–Sept. 4, 1663," *The Avalon Project: Documents in Law, History and Diplomacy*. Yale Law School: Lillian Goldman Law Library. Accessed March 1, 2016. http://avalon.law.yale.edu/17th_century/nc02.asp.

Page 35, callout quote: Herman Husband, *An Impartial Relation of the First and Causes of the Recent Differences in Public Affairs Etc*. New Bern, N.C., 1770, pp. 64–68.

Page 38, line 7: Jim Piecuch. "'Light Horse Harry' Lee and Pyle's Massacre." *Journal of the American Revolution: Online Magazine, Annual Volumes & Book Series*, (June 19, 2013). Accessed March 1, 2016. http://allthingsliberty.com/2013/06/light-horse-harry-lee-and-pyles-massacre/.

Page 39, callout quote: Hugh F. Rankin, *The North Carolina Continentals*. Chapel Hill, N.C.: University of North Carolina Press, 1971, p. 310.

Regions of the 13 Colonies		
Northern Colonies	**Middle Colonies**	**Southern Colonies**
Connecticut, Massachusetts, New Hampshire, Rhode Island	Delaware, New Jersey, New York, Pennsylvania	Georgia, Maryland, North Carolina, South Carolina, Virginia
land more suitable for hunting than farming; trees cut down for lumber; trapped wild animals for their meat and fur; fished in rivers, lakes, and ocean	the "Breadbasket" colonies—rich farmland, perfect for growing wheat, corn, rye, and other grains	soil better for growing tobacco, rice, and indigo; crops grown on huge farms called plantations; landowners depended heavily on servants and slaves to work in the fields

Select Bibliography

Frost, John. *An Illuminated History of North America*. New York: Henry Bill, 1854.

Harris, James Coffee. *The personal and family history of Charles Hooks and Margaret Monk Harris*. Rome, Ga., 1911.

Hughson, Shirley Carter. *The Carolina Pirates and Colonial Commerce, 1670–1740*. Baltimore, The Johns Hopkins University Press, 1894.

Husband, Herman. *An Impartial Relation of the First and Causes of the Recent Differences in Public Affairs Etc*. New Bern, N.C., 1770.

Johnson, Charles. *A General History of the Robberies and Murders of the Most Notorious Pyrates…* Edited by Arthur L. Hayward. New York: George Routledge & Sons, 1927.

Lawson, John. *A New Voyage to Carolina*. London: 1709. https://archive.org stream/newvoyagetocarol00laws#page/n3/mode/2up.

Lee, Robert E. *Blackbeard the Pirate: A Reappraisal of His Life and Times*. Winston-Salem, N.C.: John F. Blair, 1974.

Lefler, Hugh T., and William S. Powell. *Colonial North Carolina: A History*. New York: Scribner, 1973.

McFarlane, Anthony. *The British in the Americas 1480–1815*. New York: Longman, 1994.

Powell, William S. *North Carolina: A History*. Chapel Hill, N.C.: University of North Carolina Press, 1988.

Rankin, Hugh F. *The North Carolina Continentals*. Chapel Hill, N.C.: University of North Carolina Press, 1971.

Ready, Milton. *The Tar Heel State: A History of North Carolina*. Columbia, S.C.: University of South Carolina Press, 2005.

Salley, Alexander Samuel. *Narratives of Early Carolina, 1650–1708, Volume 12*. New York: Charles Scribner's Sons, 1911.

Stahle, David W., et al. "The Lost Colony and Jamestown Droughts." *Science* 280, no. 5363 (April 24, 1998): 564–567.

Index

10/3/17